SWEDISH SLANGUAGE

A **FUN** VISUAL GUIDE TO SWEDISH TERMS AND PHRASES BY MIKE ELLIS

GIBBS SMITH
TO ENRICH AND INSPIRE HUMANKIND

DEDICATED TO SUZANNE, VIRGINIA, MIKEY, AND PHIDGETTE

First Edition
21 20 19 18 17   5 4 3 2 1

Text © 2017 Mike Ellis
Illustrations © 2017 Rupert Bottenberg, except illustrations
of cup on pages 7, 57 © iconizer/Shutterstock.com; yeti on
page 8 © Reno Martin/Shutterstock.com; knot on pages 9,
29, 63, 87, 88 © Wiktoria Pawlak/Shutterstock.com; barn
on pages 11, 12 © Oleg Iatsun/Shutterstock.com; stop
sign on pages 16, 83 © Christophe Testi/Shutterstock.
com; duck on page 17 © Cattallina/Sutterstock.com;
foot on page 17 © IhorZigor/Shutterstock.com; golfer
on page 24 © AA39/Shutterstock.com; hand on page
26 © Peter Hermes Furian/Shutterstock.com; stairs on
page 26 © VoodooDot/Shutterstock.com; nut on page
28 © Aleks Melnik/Shutterstock.com; dot on pages 28,
31, 66; hangar on page 34 © puruan/Shutterstock.com;
apple on page 40 © Ellika/Shutterstock.com; fin on
pages 44, 55 © Bakai/Shutterstock.com; pig on page 50 ©
Sabelskaya/Shutterstock.com; ring on page 62 © natrot/
Shutterstock.com; lettuce on page 72 © Prokhorovich/
Shutterstock.com; arrow on page 76 © Omela/Shutterstock.
com; soap on page 80 © okili77/Shutterstock.com;
hotel on page 82 © 3D Vector/Shutterstock.com; dog
on pages 87, 88 © ArtHeart/Shutterstock.com.

Published by
Gibbs Smith
P.O. Box 667
Layton, Utah 84041

1.800.835.4993 orders
www.gibbs-smith.com

Designed by michelvrana.com

Gibbs Smith books are printed on paper produced
from sustainable PEFC-certified forest/controlled
wood source. Learn more at www.pefc.org.
Printed and bound in Hong Kong

Library of Congress Cataloging-in-Publication Data

Names: Ellis, Mike, 1961- author.
Title: Swedish slanguage : a fun visual guide
to Swedish terms and phrases /
   Mike Ellis.
Description: First edition. | Layton, Utah :
Published by Gibbs Smith, [2017]
   | Series: Slanguage
Identifiers: LCCN 2017004944 | ISBN 9781423647393 (pbk.)
Subjects: LCSH: Swedish language--
Conversation and phrase books--English.
Classification: LCC PD5121 .E67 2017 | DDC 439.783/421–dc23
LC record available at https://lccn.loc.gov/2017004944

CONTENTS

HOW TO USE THIS BOOK

If you have always wanted to learn the basics of Swedish, but traditional methods seemed overwhelming or intimidating, this is the book for you! Just follow the directions below and soon you'll be able to say dozens of words and phrases in Swedish.

• Follow the illustrated prompts and practice saying the phrase quickly and smoothly.

• Emphasize the words or syllables highlighted in red.

• A strikethrough means you don't pronounce that letter or letters.

• Learn to string together words or phrases to create many more phrases.

• Draw your own pictures to help with memorization and pronunciation.

Note: This book may produce Americanized Swedish.

For free sound bytes, visit slanguage.com.

GREETINGS AND RESPONSES

Hello
Hej

Hay

Good morning
God morgon

Good More Own

How are you?
Hur mår du?

Hear More Due?

How's it going?
Hur går det?

Hear Gore Debt?

Fairly well
Ganska bra

Guns Cup Bra

So so
Sådär

Sue Dar

Not too well
Inte så bra

Inn Tessa Bra

Welcome
Välkommen

Val Comb Men

Help *Hjälp*	**Yelp**
Please *Snälla*	**Snail Lot**
I'm sorry *Förlåt*	**Fur Low't**
Don't worry about it *Det gör inget*	**Day Your Inn Yeti**

Thank you
Tack

Tack

You're welcome
Ni är välkomna

Near Val Comb Knot

Cheers!
Skål!

S'Coal!

Goodbye
Hejdå

Hey Doe

Baby
Bebis

Bay Bees

Child
Barn

Barn

Couple
Par

Par

Cousin
Kusin

Coo Sin

Father
Far

Far

Grandchildren
Barnbarn

Barn Barn

Paternal grandmother
Farmor

Far More

Maternal grandmother
Mormor

More More

Grandson
Sonson

Sewn Sewn

Mother
Mor

More

Sister
Syster

Sister

Son
Son

Sewn

| Age | **Older** |
| *Ålder* | |

| Bath | **Bod** |
| *Bad* | |

| Blood | **Blowed** |
| *Blod* | |

| Cheek | **Cheen'd** |
| *Kind* | |

Cold *Förkylning*	**Fur Shilling**
Contagious *Smittsam*	**S'Mitt Sum**
To cough *Hosta*	**Hoe Stop**
Dead *Död*	**Dud**

To die
Dö

Duck

Foot
Fot

Foot

Leg
Ben

Bee Ann

Life
Liv

Live

Lipstick
Läppstift

Lap Stiffed

To lose weight
Gå ner i vikt

Goon Airy Vic

Medicine
Medicin

Medicine

Mouth
Mun

Moon

| Navel | **Novel** |
| *Navel* | |

| Nose | **NASA** |
| *Näsa* | |

| Pharmacy | **~~Top~~ Oh Tech** |
| *Apotek* | |

| Pill | **Top Let** |
| *Tablett* | |

Shoulder
Axel

Axle

Throat
Hals

Halls

To yawn
Gäspa

Yes Pa

Armchair
Fåtölj

Foe Tell Eel

Balcony
Balkong

Ball Kong

Bed
Säng

Sing

Bedroom
Sovrum

Sew Vroom

Bench
Bänk

Bank

Bookshelf
Bokhylla

Boo Kill Lot

Carpet
Matta

Ma Tough

Chair
Stol

Stole

Dishwasher
Diskmaskin

Disk Ma Quinn

Elevator
Hiss

He's

Floor
Golv

Golf

Furniture
Möbel

 Ma Bell

Garden *Trädgård*	**Tray Court**
House *Hus*	**Whose**
Kettle *Vattenkokare*	**Vat Ten Coke Care Red**
Kitchen *Kök*	**Shook**

Towel
Handduk

Hand Duke

Trash
Skräp

Scrap

Vacuum cleaner
Dammsugare

Dam Sue Gay Ray

Window
Fönster

Fun Stair

Calculator
Miniräknare

Mini Rack Nut Red

Commentary
Kommentar

Comb Men Tar

Computer
Dator

Dot Tore

Cook
Kock

Coke

Employee *Anställd*	**On Stelled**
File *Arkiv*	**Are Kiv**
Idea *Idé*	**Eee Day Ah**
Journalist *Journalist*	**Who're Knot Least**

Lawyer *Advokat*	**Add Voo Cot**
Method *Metod*	**Met Toad**
Office *Kontor*	**Cone Tore**
Philosopher *Filosof*	**Fee Low Sofa**

Physicist *Fysiker*	**Fizz See Care**
Pilot *Pilot*	**Peal Oat**
Soldier *Soldat*	**Sole Dot**

Blouse
Blus

Blues

Bracelet
Armband

Arm Band

Cotton
Bomull

Bow Moo'l

Dirty
Smutsig

Smoot Sick

Clothes hanger
Klädhängare

Clad Hangar Ray

Hat
Hatt

Hot

Pants
Byxor

Big Sore

Shoes
Skor

Score

Stain *Fläck*	**Fleck**
Tie *Slips*	**Slips**
Velvet *Sammet*	**Sum Met**
Wedding dress *Brudklänning*	**Brood Clanning**

FOOD AND RESTAURANTS

Do you have . . . ?
Har du . . . ?

Hard Due . . . ?

Yog School Love Veal

Yacht . . .

I'd like . . .
Jag skulle vilja . . .

Taste
Smak

Smock

Delicious
Utsökt

Boot Sucked

Yum
Mums

Mooms

Cheese
Ost

Owes

Dozen
Dussin

Due Sin

Egg
Ägg

Egg

To imbibe
Insupa

Inn Soup Pa

Meat
Kött

Shut

Meatball
Köttbulle

Shut Boo Let

Omelet
Omelett

Ah Moo Let

Orange
Apelsin

Apple Sin

Pair
Par

Par

Part
Del

Deal

Pastries *Bakverk*	**Bock Very**
Piece *Bit*	**Bit**
Potato *Potatis*	**Poe Tot Tease**
Salmon *Lax*	**Lax**

Sausage *Korv*	**Corvette**
Tea *Te*	**Tee**
Turkey *Kalkon*	**Cal Cone**
Weight *Vikt*	**Victor**

PLANTS, ANIMALS, AND NATURE

Bee
Bi

Bib

Camel
Kamel

Cam Me Yell

Cloudy
Molnigt

Mole Knit

Dolphin
Delfin

Dell Fin

Flower
Blomma

Blue Ma

Fog
Dimma

Dee Ma

Goose
Gås

Goes

It's windy
Det är blåsigt

Day Are Blow Sit

Mosquito *Mygga*	**Meek Yeah**
Oak *Ek*	**Eek**
Planet *Planet*	**Plan Eat**
Poplar *Poppel*	**Pope Pell**

Rabbit
Kanin

Can Inn

River
Flod

Flowed

Sea
Hav

Hovel

Seaweed
Tång

Tongue

Snow
Snö

Snow

Sun
Sol

Soul

Tiger
Tiger

Tigger

Willow
Pil

Pill

ADJECTIVES AND ADVERBS

Alone
Ensam

En Sum

Doe Lick

Bad
Dålig

Careful
Försiktig

Fur Shick Tick

Clumsy
Klumpig

K'Loom Pig

Dangerous
Farlig

Far Leak

Elsewhere
Annanstans

Announce Tans

Empty
Tom

Tomb

Enough
Tillräckligt

Till Wreck Lit

Fat *Tjock*	**Shock**
Finally *Till sist*	**Till Ceased**
Free *Fri*	**Frizz**
Good *Bra*	**Bra**

Handsome *Snygg*	**Snig**
Honest *Ärlig*	**Are League**
Impatient *Otålig*	**Oh Tall Lick**
Last *Sist*	**Ceased**

Latest
Senast

See An Us

Long
Lång

Long

Married
Gift

Yif'd

New
Ny

Knee

Noisy *Högljudd*	**Hug You'd**
Pretty *Fin*	**Fin**
Quickly *Snabbt*	**Snobbed**
Quite *Ganska*	**Gone Scott**

Rarely
Sällan

Salon

Rich
Rik

Rick

Sad
Ledsen

Less Sun

Simple
Enkel

Ankle

Single
Singel

Seen Yell

Slow
Sakta

Sock Top

Small
Liten

Lit Ten

Somewhat
Ganska

Guns Cup

Somewhere *Någonstans*	**Nun Stuns**
Still *Ändå*	**Ann Doe**
Straight ahead *Rakt fram*	**Rocked From**
Then *Då*	**Due**

Thin *Smal*	**Small**
Tranquil *Lugn*	**Loon**
Ugly *Ful*	**Fool**
Unhappy *Olycklig*	**Ooh Lick Lick**

| Usual | **Von League** |
| *Vanlig* | |

| Well | **Bra** |
| *Bra* | |

| Whole | **Heel** |
| *Hel* | |

To be wrong
Ha fel

Huff Feel

To become
Bli

Bliss

To bounce
Studsa

Stood Sock

To call on the phone
Ringa

Ring Yacht

To choose
Välja

Veil Yacht

To come
Komma

Comb Ma

To disappear
Försvinna

Fur Sheen Knot

To dress
Klä på sig

Clap Pose Say

To go down
Gå ner

Go Near

To have fun
Ha kul

Hot Cool

To hit
Slå

Slow

To hope
Hoppas

Hoe Puss

To joke
Skämta

Scam Tough

To listen to
Lyssna på

Lease Snap Poe

To meet
Möta

Ma Top

To move
Flytta

Flit Top

To offer
Erbjuda

Ear You Dot

To pull
Dra

Draw

To relax
Slappna av

Slap Now Of

To release
Släppa

Slap Pa

To reside
Bo

Boo

To run
Springa

Spring Yacht

To ski
Åka skidor

Oak Uh Squid Door

To smell
Lukta

Looked Up

To succeed
Lyckas

Lick Us

To sweep
Sopa

Sew Pa

To think
Tänka

Tank Yacht

To watch
Se på

Say Poe

According to
Enligt

Ian Lit

Against
Emot

Eh Moot

Also
Också

Oak Sew

Among
Bland

Blond

And
Och

Oak

Between
Mellan

May Long

But
Men

Men

Everybody
Alla

Allah

In order that
Så att

Sew What

Likewise
Likaledes

Leak Uh Lettuce

One more thing
En sak till

An Sock Teal

So
Så

Sew

Something *Något*	**No Got**
Them *Dem*	**Dumb**
Towards *Mot*	**Moot**
You *Du*	**Due**

To borrow	**Loan Ah**
Låna	

To buy	**Sure Pa**
Köpa	

Cash	**Cone Taunt**
Kontant	

Cheap	**Bee League**
Billig	

Coin
Mynt

Mint

Credit card
Kreditkort

Credit Court

⟹⟶

Euro
Euro

Arrow

Flea market
Loppmarknad

Lope Mark Nod

List *Lista*	**Least Ah**
Pastry shop *Konditori*	**Cone Dee Toe Ray**
Store *Affär*	**Ah Far**
Vending machine *Automat*	**Auto Mott**

TRAVEL AND TRANSPORTATION

Building *Byggnad*	**Big Nod**
Bus *Buss*	**Boost**
Bus stop *Hållplats*	**Hole Plats**
Car *Bil*	**Bill**

Castle
Slott

Slot

Driver's license
Körkort

Sure Court

Dump
Soptipp

Soap Tip

Embassy
Ambassad

Um Bass Sod

Entrance
Ingång

Inn Gong

Gasoline
Bensin

Ben Sin

Gas station
Bensinmack

Ben Sin Mack

Horn
Tuta

2 Top

Hotel
Hotell

Hotel

One-way ticket
Enkelbiljett

Ankle Bill Yet

Park
Parkera

Park Kay Rough

Path
Stig

Stigma

Postcard *Vykort*	**Vic Court**
Start a car *Starta en bil*	**Start Ann Bill**
Stop sign *Stoppskylt*	 **Stop Wield**
Supermarket *Stormarknad*	**Store Mark Nod**

Ticket
Biljett

Bill Yet

Tire
Däck

Deck

Tire pressure
Däcktryck

Deck Trick

Tow truck
Bärgningsbil

Barry Ning Spill

Trail
Spår

Spore

Train station
Tågstation

Toga Stat Hone

Truck stop
Långtradarcafé

Long Trotter Café

Day
Dag

Dog

It's noon
Det är mitt på dagen

Day Army Put Dog Inn

Midnight
Midnatt

Mid Knot

Moon Nod

Month
Månad

Night
Natt

Knot

The past
Det förflutna

Day Fur Flute Knot

Since when?
Sedan när?

Say Done Air?

Today
Idag

 E Dog

SPORTS AND ENTERTAINMENT

Cards *Kort*	**Court**
Checkers *Dam*	**Dumb**
Cinema *Bio*	**Bee Yo**
Circus *Cirkus*	**Seer Coos**

Flute
Flöjt

Fled

Luge
Rodel

Rope Dale

High jump
Höjdhopp

Head Hop

Poetry
Poesi

Poe Ess Say

Song
Låt

Flute

Sound
Ljud

You'd

Violin
Fiol

Fee Yule

To swim
Simma

See Ma

EDUCATION

File *Fil*	**Fill**
Chapter *Kapitel*	**Cap Pea Tell**
Economics *Ekonomi*	**Ache Cone No Me**
Eraser *Suddgummi*	**Sued Goo Me**

Grade
Gradera

Grub Deer Uh

Subject
Ämne

Am Net

Subtraction
Subtraktion

Sub Track Hone

Wrong
Felaktig

Fee Lock Tick

SWEDENGLISH

All the following words are identical in spelling and meaning in English and Swedish. Although you may experience small slanguage pronunciation differences, you will still be understood.

- Arm
- Avocado
- Bank
- Blond
- Clown
- Dollar
- England

- Finger
- Fort
- Full
- Golf
- London
- Lotus
- Lunch

- Mango
- Museum
- Okay
- Plus
- Pump
- Salt
- Silver

- Smart
- T-shirt
- Taxi
- Tennis
- Toast
- Video
- Zoo